West Chicago Public Library District
118 West Washington
West Chicago, IL 60185-2803
Phone # (630) 231-1552
Fax # (630) 231-1709

KRONOSAURUS

PREHISTORIC BEASTS
KRONOSAURUS

MARC ZABLUDOFF
ILLUSTRATED BY PETER BOLLINGER

Marshall Cavendish
Benchmark

New York

Published by Marshall Cavendish Benchmark
An imprint of Marshall Cavendish Corporation

Website: www.marshallcavendish.us

This publication represents the opinions and views of the author based on Marc Zabludoff's personal experience, knowledge, and research. The information in this book serves as a general guide only. The author and publisher have used their best efforts in preparing this book and disclaim liability rising directly and indirectly from the use and application of this book.

Other Marshall Cavendish Offices: Marshall Cavendish International (Asia) Private Limited, 1 New Industrial Road, Singapore 536196 • Marshall Cavendish International (Thailand) Co Ltd. 253 Asoke, 12th Flr, Sukhumvit 21 Road, Klongtoey Nua, Wattana, Bangkok 10110, Thailand • Marshall Cavendish (Malaysia) Sdn Bhd, Times Subang, Lot 46, Subang Hi-Tech Industrial Park, Batu Tiga, 40000 Shah Alam, Selangor Darul Ehsan, Malaysia

Marshall Cavendish is a trademark of Times Publishing Limited

All websites were available and accurate when this book was sent to press.

Library of Congress Cataloging-in-Publication Data

Zabludoff, Marc.
Kronosaurus / Marc Zabludoff ; illustrated by Peter Bollinger.
p. cm. —(Prehistoric beasts)
Summary: "Explore Kronosaurus, its physical characteristics,
when and where it lived, how it lived, what other animals lived
alongside it, and how we know this"—Provided by publisher.
Includes bibliographical references and index.
ISBN 978-1-60870-035-6
1. Kronosaurus—Juvenile literature. I. Bollinger, Peter, ill. II. Title.
QE862.P4Z33 2011
567.9'37—dc22
2009050575

Editor: Christine Florie
Publisher: Michelle Bisson
Art Director: Anahid Hamparian
Series Designer: Alicia Mikles

Photo research by Connie Gardner

The photographs in this book are used by permission and through the courtesy of:
Getty Images: Andy Rouse, 10; DEA Picture Library, 11; Time and Life Pictures, 18.

Printed in Malaysia (T)
1 3 5 6 4 2

CONTENTS

ANCIENT SEAFOOD

The giant rises through the water. On and on it comes, its huge head followed immediately by its broad, heavy body. It is perfectly at home in the water, but it is not a fish. It is an ancient, air-breathing **reptile** called a **plesiosaur**. It has a short neck and four large, flat flippers placed where another animal's legs might be.

As it breaks the surface, the beast's long jaws open to reveal a forest of long, heavy, pointed teeth. With its mouth open, it sucks in such great volumes of air that a breeze ripples across the water. For a moment the huge animal floats on the surface. Then its powerful flippers pull it down into the depths again, and the wide body disappears. This ancient beast, called *Kronosaurus*, has gone in search of food.

Only minutes later a second creature surfaces. It too is a plesiosaur, though of a very different kind. It is not small—it stretches 15 feet from

Kronosaurus, a short-necked plesiosaur, ate a variety of sea creatures—among them, long-necked plesiosaurs.

the tip of its narrow snout to the end of its short tail. But even so, it is less than half as long as *Kronosaurus*. Except for its four paddlelike limbs, its body is shaped differently as well. It has a much smaller head and a much longer neck, and its teeth are more like needles than knives. This new visitor from below does not spend any more time on the surface than it needs to. It fills its lungs with air, then starts to dive, on the hunt for fish.

The animal has barely begun its descent when, without warning, it is hit with the force of an erupting volcano. *Kronosaurus* has struck. Despite the long-necked plesiosaur's bulk, the attack pushes it back toward the surface as if it weighs nothing. Tremendous jaws surround its head for just an instant. Then all goes dark. The water churns violently, but the animal sees and hears nothing. In no time it has gone from hunted to hunter to a meal for one of the greatest sea creatures of all time.

THE LOOK OF A SEA MONSTER

By any measure, *Kronosaurus* was a monstrous animal. It was at least 30 to 35 feet long—as long as a three-story house is tall. Its head alone was as much as 9 feet long. That is roughly the length of a car and more than twice as long as the terrifying head of a *Tyrannosaurus rex*. Nearly the entire head was taken up by the powerful jaws, which were filled with sharp, cone-shaped teeth. Most of those teeth were immense, as long as 11 inches. With its jaws closed, *Kronosaurus*'s teeth jutted out like butcher knives over the sides of its mouth.

The huge head of *Kronosaurus* was built for attack, with strong jaws lined with long, sharp teeth.

9

Flippers similar to those of sea turtles moved *Kronosaurus* swiftly through the water.

To propel itself through the water, *Kronosaurus* used four long, tapered flippers, somewhat like the flippers of a sea turtle, though much bigger. It also had a tail, but the tail was too short to help it swim. That tail was a feature *Kronosaurus* inherited from its distant ancestors, which were animals that walked on land. But they had given up the land for a life in the water millions of years earlier. Over thousands of centuries their **descendants** gradually **evolved**, or changed, into a form better suited for life in the water. Their four legs, for example, grew broader and flatter until they became huge paddles.

Those four flippers allowed *Kronosaurus* to move easily through the sea, attacking any animal it liked. Ancient sharks were no match for its massive teeth. Neither were armored turtles or ammonites, squidlike creatures encased in a large spiral shell. *Kronosaurus* ate them all, and many other creatures as well. It even ate other animals like itself. But exactly what kind of animal was *Kronosaurus*?

Ammonites were one of the many sea creatures that *Kronosaurus* ate.

DID YOU KNOW?

The name *Kronosaurus* comes from *saurus*, meaning "lizard" or "reptile," and *Kronos*, the frightening father of the ancient Greek god Zeus. According to myth, Kronos was so worried that one of his children would overthrow him that he ate them all. Only Zeus survived, hidden by his mother.

SWIMMING TO THE TOP

**Pterosaurs, or "winged lizards,"
are not related to birds or bats.**

Kronosaurus appeared on Earth around 110 million years ago, during a time that is often called the Age of Reptiles. Today, the reptiles we are familiar with are chiefly snakes, lizards, turtles, alligators, and crocodiles. While some of these grow quite large, they are nothing like the giant reptiles of long ago. Nor do they exist in such great variety.

In *Kronosaurus*'s time the giant reptiles we know as dinosaurs dominated the land. Flying reptiles called **pterosaurs** (from the Greek words for "wing" and

During the Age of Reptiles, dinosaurs walked the land, plesiosaurs and other creatures swam the seas, and winged pterosaurs flew through the skies.

"lizard") soared and glided through the skies. Porpoise-shaped reptiles known as **ichthyosaurs** ("fish lizards") swam through the sea. With them swam the strange creatures known as the long-necked plesiosaurs (the "nearly lizards," so named because they looked more like familiar modern reptiles than did the ichthyosaurs). These were large, fish-eating reptiles with four long flippers, long necks, small heads, and slender, needlelike teeth.

These were animals whose bodies had changed remarkably from the bodies of their land-walking ancestors. They were well suited for life in the sea. But they did not become totally like fish and breathe in the water. Like today's whales—whose ancestors were land-walking, fur-covered **mammals**—ancient seagoing reptiles had to come up for air.

Among the plesiosaurs was a group of animals that, over hundreds of thousands of years, developed quite differently. Instead of long, thin necks, they grew short, thick necks. Rather than small heads filled with slender teeth, they grew large heads filled with massive teeth.

Scientists refer to these short-necked plesiosaurs as the **pliosaurs** ("more like lizards"), and *Kronosaurus* was one of them. In their time the pliosaurs were the top **predators** of the sea—no animal was big enough to threaten them, and they could dine on whatever they could catch.

Although ichthyosaurs looked somewhat like porpoises, they were neither mammals nor fish but fast-swimming, air-breathing reptiles.

ROCK-HARD EVIDENCE

The first *Kronosaurus* **fossils** were found in 1899 in Australia. They consisted of only a piece of jaw and some teeth, but that was enough for **paleontologists** to realize that the fossils had once belonged to a giant pliosaur. In 1931 fossil hunters found a more complete *Kronosaurus* skeleton buried in the Australian rocks. However, many of the bones were worn and broken. They were in even worse shape after they were removed from the ground. The rock that contained them was so hard that the discoverers used dynamite to blast it apart.

It took many years for paleontologists to put together the bones and get an idea of what *Kronosaurus* looked like. As they worked, they were forced to make guesses when bones were either missing or badly damaged. When they were finally done, the animal they constructed was 42 feet long—the biggest sea-swimming reptile ever seen.

Paleontologists first discovered *Kronosaurus* fossils in Australia in 1899.

Today, that skeleton is on display at the Museum of Comparative Zoology at Harvard University in Cambridge, Massachusetts. But most paleontologists think that rebuilt *Kronosaurus* is too long. Other fossils, such as those found far from Australia, in South America, hint that the true size of *Kronosaurus* was no more than 35 feet. Whatever its exact size, though, there is no argument over the danger this creature once posed to its neighbors. Even at this smaller size, *Kronosaurus* was the size of a school bus.

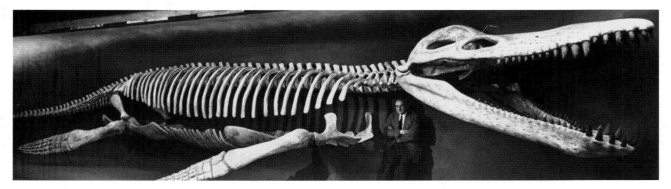

A 42-foot *Kronosaurus* is still on view at Harvard University in Cambridge, Massachusetts, but most paleontologists now think the rebuilt skeleton is at least seven feet too long.

WAS *KRONOSAURUS* THE BIGGEST ANIMAL EVER TO LIVE IN THE OCEAN?

No, though it was probably the biggest of its time. The largest pliosaur ever may have been *Liopleurodon*, which lived millions of years before *Kronosaurus*. It grew to be at least 50 feet long. Many modern whales are also longer than *Kronosaurus*, but none probably attack **prey** as large as the animals *Kronosaurus* attacked.

MONSTROUS QUESTIONS

There are many questions about *Kronosaurus* for which scientists have no certain answers. For example, was its skin rough and scaly, like a dinosaur's, or was it smooth and sleek to help its body glide through the water?

No one knows what color *Kronosaurus* was, either. Most likely, it was some combination of black, white, and gray, like today's whales. It might have been dark on top and white on the bottom, like an orca. But it could also have been striped like a tiger.

Another mystery is precisely how *Kronosaurus* swam. Sea turtles are the only living animals built anything like a pliosaur, as they, too, have four flipperlike limbs. But sea turtles move somewhat slowly, and they do not use all four flippers for swimming. They "fly" through the water by beating only their front two flippers up and down. They use the rear two flippers for steering.

Exactly how *Kronosaurus* beat its long, paddlelike flippers to move quickly through the water is still a mystery.

It is very unlikely that *Kronosaurus* swam this way. Its back flippers were enormous—at least 6 or 7 feet long—so they must have been used to generate power and speed, not just for steering. But how? Did *Kronosaurus* beat first with the front two flippers, then with the back? Did it move all four at the same time? It is difficult to find the answer, because there simply is no animal on Earth today that swims in either manner.

One last mystery concerns how a young *Kronosaurus* got its start in life. In general, lizards, alligators, turtles, and other reptiles all begin life by breaking out of an egg laid on land in a nice, warm, dry nest. Dinosaurs did also.

Some reptiles today, however, give birth to live young. Among them are several sea snakes, which spend their entire lives in the ocean. The extinct, porpoise-shaped ichthyosaurs also bore living young. Did giant pliosaurs like *Kronosaurus* find a way to avoid coming out of the water to lay eggs? Many scientists think so. They find it hard to imagine how the heavy animals could have crawled onto land. Their flippers probably were not strong enough to support their great weight out of the water.

Scientists think that *Kronosaurus* did not lay eggs but rather gave birth to live young in the water. Here a mother hunts with her offspring.

ATTACK MODE

Kronosaurus must have been a good swimmer, but it probably could not swim very fast for very long. It caught its meals after a short sprint rather than a long chase. Scientists think it hunted mostly by sight. *Kronosaurus* had large eyes and could see well underwater. But it may also have hunted by smell.

Paleontologists have found that some big pliosaurs actually had rather small nostrils—perhaps too small for taking in great amounts of air quickly. These big animals may have breathed mostly through their mouths when they rose to the surface. They may have used their nostrils mainly for detecting scents in the water, much as sharks do today.

Whether it found its prey by sight or by smell, the attack of a *Kronosaurus* must have been terrifying. When its enormous, gaping jaws snapped shut, any animal caught in its monstrous teeth would have been horribly injured.

***Kronosaurus* was a fierce hunter, crushing its prey with its powerful jaws and sharp teeth.**

Paleontologists have found a skull from a long-necked plesiosaur that is indented with what they think are *Kronosaurus* tooth marks. The skull is crushed and broken in half.

Kronosaurus swallowed small prey whole. It crushed large-shelled creatures, like ammonites, with the rounded teeth located at the back of its mouth. But if it killed a large animal, such as a 20-foot-long plesiosaur, it needed to rip it apart. It probably held on to the animal with its long, pointed front teeth while it violently twisted and thrashed until a piece broke free. Alligators and crocodiles tear their prey apart this way.

Kronosaurus was obviously a successful hunter. This mighty predator thrived in the ancient sea until it eventually became extinct, sometime after 100 million years ago. Precisely why it disappeared, no one knows. But other big plesiosaurs continued to rule the seas for many millions of years. Finally, by 65 million years ago, they too disappeared, along with dinosaurs. Other large, toothy predators would one day swim through the same oceans, but they would be fish and whales, not reptiles. When the plesiosaurs vanished, the giant sea dwellers from the Age of Reptiles were gone forever.

TIMELINE

380–375 million years ago	Four-legged animals appear.
340–310 million years ago	Reptiles appear.
240 million years ago	The first dolphin-shaped ichthyosaurs appear in the sea; long-necked, web-footed nothosaurs, possible ancestors of plesiosaurs, appear.
230 million years ago	The first dinosaurs appear.
200 million years ago	The first pliosaurs appear.
110 million–100 million years ago	*Kronosaurus* appears in the seas around Australia and South America.
100 million–85 million years ago	All ichthyosaurs become extinct; large, lizardlike, sea-dwelling reptiles called mosasaurs appear.
65 million years ago	Dinosaurs, pterosaurs, mosasaurs, plesiosaurs, and pliosaurs become extinct.
53 million years ago	The first whales appear.

GLOSSARY

descendants	all of an animal's offspring: its children, grandchildren, and so on.
evolve	to change over time.
extinct	gone forever.
fossil	the remains of an ancient animal or plant.
ichthyosaur (ICK-thee-uh-sawr)	an extinct dolphin-shaped reptile that lived in the sea.
mammal	one of the group of animals that has hair or fur, gives birth to live young, and feeds those young with milk.
paleontologist	a scientist who studies fossils to learn about the past.
plesiosaur (PLEE-see-uh-sawr)	an extinct sea-dwelling reptile with needle-sharp teeth, paddle-shaped legs, and a long neck.
pliosaur (PLEE-uh-sawr)	a relative of the long-necked plesiosaurs, with a short neck, a massive head, and large, cone-shaped teeth.
predator	an animal that hunts and eats other animals.
prey	an animal that is hunted by a predator.
pterosaur (TER-uh-sawr)	an extinct flying reptile.
reptile	one of the group of egg-laying animals that includes lizards, crocodiles, snakes, and turtles.

FIND OUT MORE

Books

Cumbaa, Stephen. *Sea Monsters: A Canadian Museum of Nature Book.* Toronto, ON: Kids Can Press, 2007.

Zabludoff, Marc. *Basilosaurus.* New York: Marshall Cavendish Benchmark, 2010.

DVD

Chased by Sea Monsters. Discovery Channel, 2003.

Websites

Oz Fossils

www.abc.net.au/science/ozfossil/

This site contains information about prehistoric creatures of Australia, including *Kronosaurus,*.

Plesiosaur Locomotion

www.plesiosauria.com/locomotion.html

Computer-animated graphics illustrate theories about how plesiosaurs swam.

Sea Monsters Fun and Games

www.nationalgeographic.com/seamonsters/kids/index.html

This National Geographic Kids website was designed to accompany the 2007 *Sea Monsters* movie.

INDEX

Page numbers in **boldface** are illustrations.

ABOUT THE AUTHOR

Marc Zabludoff, the former editor in chief of *Discover* magazine, has been involved in communicating science to the public for more than two decades. His other work for Marshall Cavendish includes books on spiders, beetles, and monkeys for the AnimalWays series, along with books on insects, reptiles, and the largely unknown and chiefly microscopic organisms known as protoctists. Zabludoff lives in New York City with his wife and daughter.

ABOUT THE ILLUSTRATOR

Peter Bollinger is an award-winning illustrator whose clients include those in the publishing, advertising, and entertainment industries. Bollinger works in two separate styles, traditional airbrush and digital illustration. He lives in California with his wife, son, and daughter.